STRONG STARTS IN THE MIND

Darsh is eloquent and emotional,
without falling into sentimentality.
Many books make you feel better;
this one makes you be better.
(Jodi Jordan)

This book will feed your mind and your
heart no matter where you are in life!
Fantastic read for all ages!
(Kathrine Zervakis)

Inspiring, thoughtful, intelligent and sharp, this book will challenge and change you
if you let it. Get it! You'll be glad you did. I keep going back to it over and over.
(Jacob P. Ray)

Darsh writes beautifully with humor,
wisdom borne from living bravely,
and a keen eye fixed on experiences
that touch us all.
(Carol Richmond)

Pages full of inspiration. The type of book you
can pick up, read a few pages and it will make
your day. Instant motivation.
(Donna Dyson)

Are you the person you've always wanted to be?

Most people aren't, and that's okay! We are all looking to improve. We want to be better parents, better siblings, better children, better employees, etc. We want to get stronger at everything.

One of the most important lessons I've learned (and that I'd like to share with you) is that "strong" as a concept is not limited to the gym or the trail or the workplace or a gender. Strong is a concept that starts in our minds. Then, in a back and forth dance with action, we learn and improve and become stronger.

This book is intended to help you on your journey to strong. 50 essays to orient your mindset and get you moving. It's a continuation of the work I started in LIVE LIKE THAT.

Start flipping through right now. You don't have to go in order. The important thing is that you begin now, because strong starts in the mind.

Thanks,
Lisbeth

If you want to read more of my work, check out www.wordswithlisbeth.com That's where some of these essays found their start, and where you'll find hundreds of inspirational posts.

Tell me what you think! Email: lisbeth.darsh@gmail.com
-- I'd love to hear your stories and if I've helped in any way.

Strong Starts In The Mind

Start It Up, Let's Go

When I was 16, I totaled the family sedan. Luckily, I did not substantially injure myself or my sister or the passengers of the other car. The day after the crash, my Yankee mother marched me outside to our remaining car. She was full of love but also steadfastly practical.

"Get in." She pointed to the driver's door.
I was young and, as you can imagine, rather scared.
"I can't," I said, "I wrecked our car yesterday. I sent Holly to the hospital."
"She's fine," said my mother. "Bruised ribs. Nothing major. Everyone is fine."
She gestured again. "Get in. You're driving."

"But--"

She waved me off. I knew better than to say another word.

"If you don't drive today, right now," she said, "it will take you longer
to get over this. Drive now. Move on. What else are you going to do?
Not drive for the rest of your life?"

I swallowed hard and reached for the door handle. I knew she was right,
but that didn't mean I wanted to do what needed to be done. I slid behind
the wheel. My mother got in on the passenger side and closed her door.

"Start it up," she said. "Let's go."

And I did. And I do, even now in life. When something goes wrong,
I wake up the next day and get back in the driver's seat.
Cold? Or phenomenally practical? Healthy?
I don't know. And I'm not sure how anyone else sees it.
This is the way I live my life. It works pretty well.

Drive. Crash. Survive. Learn. Drive again.
Start it up. Let's go.

Strong Starts In The Mind

There's no clearer way to say it: "Strong" starts in the mind. That is, the act of getting strong doesn't start in the gym. It starts in your head.

But the trouble is in the application, as it is with everything in life.

See, you can't really sit there and get super strong in your mind and then go out and tackle a lift, or love, or life and expect everything to go well. You can't research everything about the squat and then get under the bar and perform absolutely perfectly. You have to learn, get under the bar, learn some more, get under the bar, make mistakes, get back under the bar, fail horribly and get back under the bar.

Learning is a back and forth thing. It's a dance. A really complicated dance full of horrible movement at times and maybe horrendous music. But you keep going. Sometimes you get a great teacher, sometimes a horrible teacher, and sometimes the teacher is absent and you have solo practice. And, honestly, once in a while the teacher might metaphorically beat the snot out of you. (Thanks, life.) But you keep going and learning.

Strong starts in the mind, but it certainly doesn't end there or stay there. So the next time you find yourself only sitting there and trying to solve everything independent of movement or experience, maybe it's time to get up and do something. You'll be surprised at how much clearer your mental picture gets.

Even The Clouds Are Below Me

Nobody can put the blues inside me.
Nope. Not happening.

These are the days when I say to the world: "Take your anger, your bitterness, your foul mood and go peddle it elsewhere. I will not buy your brand of unhappiness today."

See, I got a barbell. And I got some bumpers. Which means I got me.

When those bumpers slide onto that bar, every burden on my back grows wings and takes flight. Things that weighed me down begin to vanish, disappearing like moths rising to some flame. Only the black rubber weights sink me now, and still you know, like the sun every single day, I will rise.

Chest up. Elbows up. Look straight ahead. Face the day. Face the shooter. Face the world.

Doesn't matter who's trying to smack me down. I can't be touched. My spirit is so high that you need extra oxygen to breathe up here.

I got my barbell. And I got me.

Ain't nobody going to put the blues inside me.

Trust

People will reveal themselves to you. Pay attention when this happens.

Don't be distracted by the lighting, or the jokes, or the colors.
Ignore the salty taste of your food. They are telling you who they are
with each gesture, each act, each look, more so than by their words.

Pay attention.

Pay attention to how they speak without words. Pay attention to what
they seem to be trying to get you to do. Pay attention, and then huddle
with the ones who are not trying but who are just being.
(Only these folks can you trust, although you do not know it yet.)

When we make mistakes in life, when we fail at something, in our
post-mortem assessment of the deal/relationship/event we often find
ourselves saying something like "I knew it. Something didn't feel right."
But we proceeded anyway.

So many of us have lost touch with our instincts. We've tried to override
our gut feelings with our brains. It doesn't work. Trust me. I tried for
so long. But this I know for sure: the older I get, the more I listen to my
gut instinct. And the more I listen to my instinct, the closer I am to free,
the closer I am to me.

Good luck.

Brave And Strong And True

Stop hiding. Stop cowering. Stop being afraid.
Stand up. Step forth. Speak out.

What is the worst that could happen if you spoke your mind? If you lived
the life you want to live?

You could be shunned, ignored, de-loved. (There is no such thing as de-loving.
It means they never really loved you to begin with. This may be painful,
but it is truth and you need to know it.)

You will survive your season of being cast out. I have.
And so have many others.

Will you be killed? If yes, then still I say "So what?" (I am a stubborn soul.)

Malala, the schoolgirl (and Nobel Prize winner) shot in the head by the
Taliban, said this: "I told myself, Malala, you have already faced death.
This is your second life. Don't be afraid -- if you are afraid, you can't move
forward."

She has guts. Where are yours? Do you have less nerve than a schoolgirl?
continued ...

Stand up.

You don't have to live this life this way.

You were once brave and strong and true. What happened to that person? Who stole her away? But, more importantly, why did you let them take her? And how can you get her back? (She is important, far more important than you realize. Find her.)

What is there to lose by being bold? Your fear. Maybe your pride. You will survive the loss of either or both. I have.

This life does not belong only to the strong, but also to those who persevere.

"Once more unto the breach, dear friends, once more."
Shakespeare, Henry V

Beacons

I wasn't feeling very strong one morning at the 6am class. It was cold,
and I was on my third day of workouts. As I walked over to the waist-high
pile of bumpers, it seemed like every person there could hear my bones creak.
I felt ancient. Instead of grabbing a pair of 25lb bumpers, I reached for the
15lb bumpers. Big George was standing there. He's got a good foot on my
height and about 15 years on my age. The hair that he has left is pure white.

"I don't think I have it in me this morning, George" I said, in way of an excuse,
like I needed to be absolved by someone.

George looked straight at me. His voice was kind but firm, like the grand-
father that he is.

"You've got to find it, Lisbeth. You're a beacon."

I barely looked up. "I feel old, George. I'm tired."

"Lisbeth, people look to you. You're a beacon."

I started to walk away with my light bumpers, still swishing my feet in
self-pity. Then I stopped and turned back. I grabbed the 25's and threw
them on my barbell. Warmed up, felt good. Did the workout. Felt great.
Much better than if I had stuck with my lesser weight, with my sad
underestimation of myself, with my self-pity, with my tiredness.

L.D.

All because George saw the light in me when I didn't even see it in myself. Because sometimes it only takes one person to believe, and you can believe too.

But I know life isn't always that simple. The lessons aren't always that clear. The path isn't always well-lit or apparent or safe. Sometimes, you don't see any path at all, so you have to make your own.

Why am I telling you this? Because I remember listening to an Indigo Girls' song one day in my twenties and hearing this lyric: "If the world is night, shine my life like a light."

The world is night sometimes. A lot of times. And so we need more light, more beacons, and more Georges. Like Edith Wharton wrote so many years ago: "There are two ways of spreading light: to be the candle or the mirror that reflects it." So, don't fold your cards, don't fold your heart, don't tuck your spirit away. Stay in the game. Together is the only way any of us find the way home.

Names

People ask this question: "What would you do if you knew you could not fail?"

I answer, "Why would I want to live a life of certainty? I want to be alive."

Risk, chance, failure, success. Of course, most things of worth sit on the other side of fear.

I wanted to name my second son "Chance." I was voted down. "Sounds like a dog's name."

I said, "Sounds like opportunity."

They didn't hear me, perhaps because I never spoke those words aloud. My fault.

"Prosper" was the other name I chose. (I had a distant relative named Prosper. I can't remember if he ever made it to America.) But that name never made it out of caucus either. So, we picked a sturdy, conventional name for our second boy: Sam. That's okay. In fact, it was perfect. He's so different that a good and basic name is exactly what he needed.

Chance and Prosper: the boys who lived only in my head, oh but what rich and fabulous lives they lived. Like the life I lived for myself in my head, far richer than anything anyone else could have dreamed for me.
continued ...

(And by rich, I don't mean wealthy. Just rich in every way that this world has yet to establish numbers or a value system, because how can you really put a value on love or happiness or soul? What numbers can you put on things beyond numbers?)

We work so hard on the things that people can see -- this car, that house, that office -- when perhaps the most important things we will ever touch are the things we cannot physically touch. A heart. A mind. A soul.
I guess it's just easier to put your eyes on a shirt or a body than a soul.

Yet these tangible things we want, so desire, so long and yearn and almost moan out loud for in our days (if we were more adventurous perhaps we would and the ache would have voice outside of our heads), these things don't really matter. People matter, and how we treat people. Life is so simple and yet not so simple at all.

Better we should really live while we live. When my sister was dying, she said, "I'm just trying to stay alive." It was all she had the strength left for. Her name was Lynn.

You Are On Your Way

Rejoice! You are on your way.

These troubles? These hardships? These struggles?

They're signs. Good signs, although they don't seem so right now.

I know they seem harsh and horrible, irrefutable proof of an unforgiving and cruel world.

But they are lessons. Hard lessons you don't want to learn, would rather not learn, would love to run away from.

They are important.

Steel isn't forged in cool waters, or on a beach with a Corona in hand, or on a bed watching Netflix. Steel is iron held in high heat. It burns before it strengthens.

And this is you, whether you want it to be or not.

What can I say to help you in this troubled time? What can I tell you that will offer some balm to your wounds, some aloe to your burns, some relief to your soul?

L.D.

Nothing but this: you have survived more than this. You will survive more than this. Take heart in these simple words, in these simple truths.

You are stronger than you know.

You can always take far more than you think you can take. The hardest part is actually within your own head.

Stop the chattering in your mind. Quiet the self-deprecation. Don't believe your own voice that brays to you daily of your unworthiness.

Believe you are worthy of great things. This is the only path that will lead you where you wish to go.

Believe you are worthy of love. You will find none until you know this. Believe you are worthy of respect. You will engender none until you realize this.

Believe you are worthy of companionship. You will receive harsh and hollow friendship until you accept this.

Long ago, James Baldwin wrote, "Our crown has already been bought and paid for. All we have to do is wear it."

Wear the crown.

Rejoice. You are on your way.

On Healing

What's worse than injury? Fear of injury. An injury will hurt. It will set you back. It might even cripple you for a while. But the fear of injury can cripple you for far longer.

Injuries happen. Everywhere. In any sport. In regular life, too.

Who hasn't tripped and fallen in their own house? Cut themselves with a sharp blade making dinner? Maybe you've also torn up your knee on the softball field, or broken your collarbone when you went over your handlebars. You've probably torn up your hands with too many pull-ups, or maybe tweaked your shoulder with a heavy clean and jerk.

Life, done right, is a contact sport. It hurts and you don't always come away with the ball and a clear path to the hoop. Sometimes, you find yourself limping off the court for a while. Time to heal and get stronger again. Important healing will need to take place between your ears, also. If you don't get your mind right after an injury, you will never get your body back to where you were, or beyond that stage.

So, learn from your injury. Be smart. But get over it. What holds most people back is their fear of pain, not pain itself. It's a mind game, and they lose. Don't be most people. Be stronger, in mind and body.

All The Best People

All the best people fall in love with the world.
All the best people hurt like you do.
All the best people taste the salt of their own tears.
And they keep going.

All the best people see the beauty of this world -- really see and feel it
-- the beauty and the glory and the ugliness and the pain and the sorrow,
all the best people continue to open their hearts.

They bleed. They hurt. They breathe and go on.

All the best people stand back up and fight like hell.

No matter what anyone has told you in this life, no matter how they
hurt you or cut you down to size, no matter what they did to you, know
this: you have the opportunity to be one of the best people ever.

As long as you're breathing, you have this chance.

Stand back up. Now. And become the person you've always wanted to be.
All the best people do.

That's The Wrong Question

"Who do they want me to be?" is the wrong question.

They.
Not you.
"Who do they want me to be?"
Don't ask that question.
Or, if you find yourself asking it, run.
Run fast.
Run a 5K.
Run to the moon.
Run anywhere.
Run back to yourself.
But always remember this: you are not here to be anybody else's anything.
You are here to be you.
You better get going on that.

Some Weeks Suck

Some weeks just suck. I'm not going to lie, or sugarcoat, or tell you to look for the good in the bad.

Some days are bad, and sometimes you get a whole week of those days.

There's not much you can do about it. Grit your teeth and finish that ride.

Not every day will be your day. Not every workout will feel good. Not every joke is going to make you laugh, and some jokes are going to make you want to punch somebody.

But don't punch. Lift. Run. Breathe. Survive.

Because tomorrow might be your day. And next week?
It might be the best ever.

Our happiness ultimately lies not in the outcome of each thing we do, but in our outlook after each thing we do.

Some things will become victories. Rejoice.
Some things will be utter failures. Learn.

continued ...

Some things will fill no one's soul but our own, and yet still they will be the rain we so needed after a very long and silent drought. Just the drops we hear on the rooftop bring us a joy that no one else can understand. That's okay. Rejoice in that rain. Rejoice in that relief.

And when the bad weeks come (which they will, because darkness can no more be conquered than the coming of night), remember that the moon rises too. It provides a little light, and that might be enough to carry you through until the sunrise.

So, on the weeks that suck, look for the moon. Her glow is subtle and you'll have to trust your footsteps more than your eyes on this path, but you can still find your way.

Build Your Own World

Someone has let go of your tether. A lover or a parent or a company.
A connection that meant so much suddenly detached and you are tumbling
head over heels in a fall without bottom yet.

And this freefall is so disconcerting -- so sudden, so frightening -- that you
think about going back to those who let go. You think about climbing
back into some pit of what feels like safety to you.

Why?

Why go back? There's nothing for you there. Whoever has let you go, they
told you nothing of your value, just that *you* were not of value to *them*.
This is their opinion, nothing more. And it really has nothing to do with you.
Do not confuse opinion with worth, or you will be doing the math of fools.

You have been handed FREEDOM. Be smart with it. Be bold with it.

Be reckless and mad and passionate and all the things you were hesitant
to be in your old life. Be that. Prove your worth not to them, but to yourself.
Build your own world.

≫

Going To Graceland

Ever go someplace just for the hell of it? That's how I ended up sliding cash under a bulletproof glass window at a decrepit motel near Graceland. When you're 23, you don't always make good decisions.

It all started on a Saturday morning at the Taco Bell in Rantoul, Illinois, about 400 miles north of Memphis, Tennessee. I was a young Air Force officer, eating burritos with my buddies after a hard night of drinking. And that's when Joe said, "We should go see Elvis."

Now, my big black lab was named Elvis, so Pat (the blonde buzz-cut lieutenant sitting at the table with us) assumed we were going to my house to hang out and watch bad movies and nurse our hangovers.

But that's not what Joe meant at all.

"Like Graceland. Where Elvis lived. Where he's buried. Let's go. It can't be more than 500 miles. We could make it there by nightfall. We come back tomorrow. We get here in time for class on Monday morning."
We were young officers with no commitments other than to our aircraft maintenance classes. The hardest part of the trip was going to be getting someone to watch my dog.

About 5pm that night, we pulled into Memphis. We found a cheap motel first, and then the liquor store. (We had learned through experience the opposite order was poor planning.)

We were also self-schooled in the art of splitting apart a motel room bed so one person got the mattress, one person got the bed springs, and one person got the floor. Pat drew the floor, although all surfaces were equally disgusting. But we were in Memphis and we weren't planning to be in our motel other than for a couple of hours in the morning after the bars closed.

One thing I learned that night was that seedy motels are stingy with their towels. And that if a towel is really thin and threadbare and small like a hand towel, you actually can slide it through that opening under a bullet-proof window. (Amazing, right? I was stunned when the clerk did it.)

But my point here isn't to tell you about bad motels or bad decisions. Sure, we ended up in a bar with an Elvis impersonator, then at some street music festival with a woman who kept flashing the crowd even though she probably should have tucked those things away when she started drawing her Social Security check. Finally, we danced in cages at some gay bar because we had told our taxi driver we wanted the best dance club in Memphis and so he brought us there. (It had taken us a short while to realize what was going on. "There only seem to be men here. Where are the girls?") And, in the morning on a few hours of sleep, we rolled into Graceland and saw the Jungle Room, then bought all sorts of wonderfully tacky Elvis memorabilia.

We had a fabulous time. And that's my point. Sometimes, you shouldn't plan. You shouldn't forecast. You shouldn't weigh and evaluate and judge and decide. Sometimes, you should just GO.

Listen to your friend's wild idea. Get in the car. Hit the gas. Don't look back. Grab that boy. Kiss that girl. Get that mohawk. Life holds so many expectations. We hold so many expectations. So many shoulds. So many musts. So many gottas. But sometimes you gotta toss the gottas. And go with what the hell instead. This life is short. Your memory is long.

I'll always remember Graceland.

Create Joy

There is so much sadness in our world. Shootings, anger, hate. We all have so many questions for which there are no answers.

The more I ponder, the more I realize there is a simple way each of us can make this world better: Create joy.

Crazy, right? Serious times demand serious answers. If you really think about it, though, joy *is* a serious answer. You can fight darkness with darkness, but do not expect light to arise from it. Instead, create light. As Marianne Williamson wrote: "The antidote to what is fundamentally wrong is the cultivation of what is fundamentally right."

Do what you can. Use what you have. Make things better for one person. Then two. And three, ten, a hundred, one thousand -- and so on, until you can go no further.

Create joy, one person at a time. Start with yourself.

That sounds selfish, doesn't it? Start with yourself? Isn't this life about service to others? It is, but in order to serve others, you must first take care of yourself.

continued ...

Sleep right, eat right, get to the gym. Get on the pull-up bar. Get on the barbell. Make the ground move fast beneath your feet. Get your body right, your heart right, your head right. Create joy within yourself.

And then spread that joy.

When people notice your life is better -- that you're happier and more fun and full of more energy -- tell them why. Tell them it all started with the pull-up bar and the barbell. Maybe they'll want to try it too.

Create joy.

Watch the light spread. Get out there and make joy happen.

Tell It To The Barbell

We go crazy if we don't tell our stories, our fears, and our secrets.

This is the source of madness: the unsprung spring. Untold stories bubble inside you, and not in a gentle way. You feel like you are drowning, because your story is everywhere inside you and nowhere outside you. And a dammed story is for the damned. That water will eventually kill you. You must break the dam.

To avoid this fate that you do not want (believe me, you do not want it, even if you have spent years convincing yourself that you do), you must talk. Some folks talk to friends, some people talk to pets, some talk to the page, and the religious talk to God. Do whatever you need to, but tell your story to someone. Rosanne Cash has a great line: "When you're a broken bird, tell Heaven."

But, if you are not religious (or even if you are), I offer this:

Tell the barbell. Tell it with your muscle and your sinew and your tendons and your synapses. And your slow reflexes that established at birth that athletic domination would never be yours. Tell the barbell.

Tell who you hate (because you do, although you try so hard not to). Tell why you can't yet forgive. (Be honest.) Tell whose voodoo doll you still want to stick with the sharp pins, again and again. (We are all human. The desire should not be confused with the act.)

Tell whose voice you still want to hear over your shoulder, suddenly in your air and space, crowding your own sense of you, their hot breath seeming to completely warm your cold being, in a way they never knew because you never ever told them and you should have, oh you should have, why didn't you tell them?

Tell your hurt, your pain, your anguish, your burdens. Tell it all. Put it into the steel and the rubber. Then lift it all from the floor to your shoulders and overhead.

Raise your burdens as high as you can reach, sink under the weight of them, feel their dominion over you. Know they could crush you.

Realize all of this.

Then let them drop. See your burdens freefall through the air, and plunge. Let the bar drop. Let it hit the ground. See it bounce up. Stand back so it does not hurt you, but guide it with your hands so that it does not hurt anyone else.

And let it clatter onto the ground.

It has no meaning -- it is just steel and rubber -- unless you pick it up again. Same as your pain and anger. Don't pick it up again. You are more intelligent than that. Leave your burdens where they lay. Walk away. Out into the world. Let the door shut behind you. See only the sun, and feel the incredible lightness of your own footsteps.

Decide To Win

Disappointment has a long half-life. It continues to exist for what seems like eons. That's the bad news.

If you fail to perform to your own expectations, you will be haunted. At least most of us will be. Those content with mediocrity or failure? Not so bothered. That's why they don't rise above, fight their way back, and succeed. Less than their best effort is okay with some people. Wish these folks well, but remember they are not you. They do not understand.

But if you've got a winner's heart, a successful soul, a burning desire to be more than you're sure you can be, you will have some sleepless nights. You will see the ghosts of your failures, and you will recognize that aching soul of defeat when you see it in other bodies.

So, what to do? Do what you've always done. Sit back after the defeat and think. Analyze.

continued ...

Brutally and honestly assess your own performance. What went right, what went wrong, what you can learn to do better next time -- whether the failure was in your workout, a competition, your job, or your relationship. Whether you failed at a lift or you failed with your child, you can learn from what happened and do better -- be better -- next time.

What's the difference between winners and losers?

Winners did the work to figure out why they lost, and then they fought like hell to improve.

Disappointment can be a fantastic catalyst, if you know how to use it. Harness that energy. Decide to win, and do what needs to be done.

Never More Beautiful

A woman is never more beautiful than when she is strong.

There's something about a woman showing strength and confidence that is sexy and arresting to many people. Whoever you are, man or woman, the image of a strong woman will provoke a reaction. Sometimes, this is positive, but sometimes there is a backlash.

Love strong women or hate strong women: you can have your opinion but really it doesn't matter. You can't change what is. That's like trying to change the sun: pure folly.

And if the image of a strong woman bothers you? Then you really need to look closer. Look at what upsets you. Look hard. Why does it anger you? What threat is it to you? And ask yourself: what are you afraid of?

L.D.

The Balance Sheet Of Your Life

By the time you get to my point in life, you've seen a lot, done even more,
and maybe didn't make all the best decisions. But, ultimately, you're hoping
that balance sheet of life is in your favor. You hope that for all the damage
you've done over the course of your confused and confusing life, somehow
you managed to do more good than harm during your time on this Earth.

Life adds up.
Actions add up.
Anger adds up.
Love adds up, too.
You know this.

There is nothing we do in this life that does not have its own accounting
or reckoning. I firmly believe that we do pay for our sins, but maybe
not in the Biblical way. I think we pay in the human, day-to-day way.
I don't fear God at the Pearly Gates like I fear my neighbors here on Earth.
If I am unkind, then unkindness will be shown to me. If I am fearful,
then I will find others fear me. If I am hateful, then hate will follow me.
And this keeps me on what some folks might call the "straight and narrow"
although I am neither straight nor narrow. Wislawa Szymborska wrote
in her poem "Possibilities" of a "cunning kindness" and perhaps this is that.

I am not simplistic, but I think life is pretty simple in some respects --
and that means in love and hate and accountability.

L.D.

And so I wish that more people saw the usefulness in compassion. This does not mean I give to get (I see no honor in that) but that my desire to keep my feet on the path of whatever righteousness I have chosen in this moment is a tad guided by my fear of a light slap from the Universe saying "Pay attention! This is not the best use of you." (Perhaps the influence of those grammar school nuns will never leave me.)

Why do I tell you this?

For no other reason than knowledge hoarded is knowledge wasted. Share what you know. Live your life so that harm is a little column on the balance sheet of your life, but good spreads across the page and onto many, many others.

»

Where You Look Is Where You'll Go

"Where you look is where you'll go." I found myself saying that to my son one day as he learned to ride a bicycle ... at the age of 14. When your kid is unique, some things come on their own time table. One of my sons learned to ride a bike at 3. One son learned at 14. Neither is better than the other. They both just are.

Kids don't learn on our timeline; they learn on their timeline. Adults are often like that too, although we try to pretend otherwise.

There is no set rule or time by which we all have to do anything, except get born and get dead. Those are the two finite points of our lives. Everything betwixt is in flux. Always has been, always will be. We only fool ourselves into thinking otherwise.

But one thing is fairly certain: where you look is where you'll go, on a bike or in this life. So pick your line well and stop riding your brakes. Fear is not your friend, but momentum is. The bumps will still be there, you just won't feel them as much. Concentrate on the delicious sensation of wind on your skin, and keep pedaling. Because, of course, movement is where we find ourselves again.

Ballaſt

"We'll be who we are, and not who we were."
Rosanne Cash, 50,000 Watts of Common Prayer.

What a universal longing: this desire to be who we really are, and to be free of who we were. Everyone wants this on some level. I don't know a soul who is unencumbered with regret. No person breathes without the inhale of miſtakes made.

But, remember this: no hot air balloon ſteers a proper course without ballaſt. A certain amount of heaviness can help with ſtability.

And so we go on, as we muſt, as we are compelled to even in the darkeſt of nights, when we sit and clutch the blankets in the cold silence, waiting to see the moon retreat, hoping it will give us a breather and then a few glorious rays of sunshine to warm us, if only for a moment. It's enough.
It has to be right now.

The night, like ballaſt, serves its purpose. Let it.

The Chasm Of Suffering

Much of our unhappiness is created by the gulf between our expectations and our reality. Much of our suffering lies in this chasm: a chasm of suffering that does not have to exist.

Can you see that? The chasm of suffering lies where our expectations do not match the reality of our situation.

We cause much of our own pain.

We expect, we anticipate, we create hurt where perhaps none had to grow. And we do it so often.
(We all do. I am no more immune to this force than you are.)

Think of the expectations you have right now for yourself and for the people in your life.

"Expectations? Of course I have expectations!" you may bristle. I get it. I used to be that way. My expectations were high, so high that no one could reach them, not even me. And I was miserable, because I confused expectations with standards. Standards are crucial for your own compass and behavior, but expectations drive you into the chasm of suffering.

Think about it. Expectations are beliefs you hold that something will happen. *Beliefs you hold.* Beliefs you have about what others will/should/can do. Sounds a bit like judgment, perhaps? Does this make sense now?
continued ...

When we establish beliefs about something totally out of our control (the behavior of others) then we create this chasm in which suffering can grow, because we cannot truly control the behavior of others any more than we can control the rising and setting of the sun.

But think about this too: what would happen if (instead of expecting) we lived in our reality? What if we didn't create a gulf between reality and our expectations? What if we simply lived where we are?

I'm not saying this is the answer to everything. But what if we didn't create a chasm of suffering? What if we tossed our expectations and stayed grounded in our reality? What would happen then?

Maybe it's an experiment worth trying.

If It Happened To You

When the results aren't favorable, few people want to accept personal responsibility.

Came in fifth on the workout? "Those other guys are beasts. Born that way."
Lose a job? "My boss sucks. I got screwed."
Break up with a girlfriend? "She's a bitch."
Slip on a sidewalk? Hurt yourself working out? Yeah, you know what comes after these accidents: more finger pointing.

But why? Why the excuses? Why play the blame game?

Because it feels better. More gratifying to your ego, easier to swallow. It wasn't your fault. You couldn't have stopped it. You didn't fail, somebody failed you.

Or perhaps it is your fault, in some way. You failed. You need to try harder. You need to do better. If it happened to you, then you were involved.

Think about this possibility, even when it's something like your girlfriend cheating on you, or your boss deciding who gets laid off, or that deadlift slipping out of your hand. If it happened to you, then you did it.

Listen and learn, or pass it off. This decision point hits you constantly in life. But how you react determines the quality of your life.

Why You Should Love A Woman Who Loves The Barbell

Because we're real.

Because our thumbs hurt from hookgripping deadlifts, and our voices are all sexy from yelling for somebody trying to pull 250 pounds from the floor when it's just not moving. We don't care. We yell anyhow, like our volume can lift pounds.

Because our posterior chains are amazing. We work like mofos to build bodacious booties and we're not afraid to talk about them. We look great heading into a room and even better leaving one. You will stare and we're okay with that. Unless you're a creep, and then we're going to get right in your grill.

Because we spit when we run. And not dribbles. We can nail that stop sign if we need to.

We know how to hug: long, well, and hard enough that your soul feels refilled and you know that you can go on simply because another human being really gives a damn about you.

We know how to listen. We've heard it all, but still your story is new. We've never heard it quite that way. And we know the right words that will help.

L.D.

We get the pain. We've lived the pain. We don't expect it to go away, ever. And we know how to deal with it. We prescribe power cleans for broken hearts.

We know to rub chalk on our calluses, but not all over our hands. We never clap and make a big cloud like they do in videos. That's not us.

We wear yoga pants, but hardly ever to yoga. We wear them to front squat, back squat, snatch, deadlift, clean and jerk, and pretty much everything else, including going to work, school meetings, doctor's appointments, and almost everywhere but weddings and funerals. And we don't give a damn if anybody says we shouldn't. Dress yourself. We'll dress us.

Because we have attitude, and we own it. There are no apologies to be given for speaking our minds, speaking our hearts, or standing up for what we believe in.

And we believe in more weight on the bar, more depth to your squat, less ice in your whiskey, and more love in your heart.

And we're not afraid to throw our clothes on the floor and stride off to the bedroom in full house lights just to get your attention. We're not ashamed of our bodies, we are only ashamed of this world for trying to put fear and self-loathing on us.

So if you can get your act together, you should love a woman who loves the barbell. Because it's not too late to really start living.

Jumping The Curb

"Will you still be there when I jump the curb?"

If you've ever taught a teenager to drive a car, you know this look in their eyes. They know you love them when the car is on hard pavement, but what they really want to know is if you'll still love them when they mess up, when they crash, when the car jumps the curb.

And you should still love them. You should be there even if the car keeps going and hits another vehicle or a building.

Let them know this. Let them know that you will be there for them no matter where the car goes. Life is hard enough with a cheering section and a safe zone. Don't make it any harder.

Quite simply, we should be there when the people we love jump the curb. Teenagers or not. Blood relatives or not. If we care about someone, we should be there when the tires are not on the pavement, the road is bumpy, and the wheel is spinning like crazy even as hands frantically try to steer out of a mess.

continued ...

And, if we are not there when they jump the curb, then we must we answer a question we were avoiding all along: Do we really love them?

"But," you say, "Enough is enough. I must hold those standards. I must teach my children/friends/loved ones that they earn respect." But I'm not talking about respect. I'm talking about love. Unconditional love. It's so horribly hard to have. I get that.

Unconditional love is a heart breaker. Unconditional love can wreck you. Unconditional love can blow a hole wider in your soul than any tape could ever measure. Yet unconditional love is also perhaps the strongest thing this world has ever known. And the strongest people have it.

The only question that remains: how strong are you? And that answer may lie over the curb.

Find Them

There are people who say honesty is overrated. They are wrong. And you shouldn't listen to them. Just because they have given up on life doesn't mean you should give up too.

Honesty is not overrated.
Neither is professionalism.
Or integrity.
Or love.
Or kindness.

Don't sit near the jaded, who neither glow nor help. Their cynical laughter is the most temporary of balms. You cannot get warm enough to heal here. You are wasting your time. Their anger holds them back, but it need not hold you back too.

Move on.

Find the ones who kept their fire, despite the cold and dark shoved at them from many pushing hands. Find the ones who could see when others could not. Find the ones who neither twirled nor spun, with no need to trick or overpower or even get anyone else to agree. In fact, they cared not whether you understood or agreed with them. They knew what they had to do.

The truly aware have no need for applause. They can't even hear it at times, so loud is the ticking of the clock inside them, so focused are they on the path in front of them that they know they must walk, walk, walk, until they are done and exhausted and full of the cheer that only the journey could provide. They know this is what they must do. They are focused. They are the ones with strength. They are the ones who can help you.

Find them.

Make This Day The Best You Can

This is where it gets hard. You're a little behind on your workout, your work, your nutrition plan, your schoolwork, your parenting, your bills, your life. So much to do, so many people to please, so little sleep. I know. I'm right there with you. Here's where you're expecting I will give a rah-rah speech.

Well, not exactly. Not today.

You know what you need to do. Underneath all the opinions that you take in from the rest of the world, there's a quiet you that knows what to do. Listen to the quiet you, and stop making yourself miserable.

Here's a simple recipe: if what you're doing to make yourself happy is actually making you sad, stop. Do something else for a while. The good people in your life won't judge you. And the folks who will judge you? Better for them to step up now and identify themselves. Clearing out old shirts in your closet creates room for new ones.

Do what you need to do for you, and let life settle itself out. That might mean going to the gym, or it might mean taking a nap, or it might mean doing absolutely nothing for an hour except listen to the rain through an open window or play checkers with a little boy who's been patiently waiting.

The world will keep spinning. And who knows? Maybe doing some power cleans will clear your brain, and that solution at work will seem pretty clear. Or maybe you'll awake from that nap in love with the world again. All you can do is make this day the best day you can. So do that. It will be enough.

≫

Dumping The Heavy Rocks

You don't remember the exact moment when you decided to stop taking it.
All the bullshit in this life, that is. When you decided to stop being a good
girl or boy. When you decided you had only one life so you might as well
live it for you, not for anyone else. (Living as someone else wishes you to
-- it even sounds silly, doesn't it? Like you would wish that on anyone else.
You wouldn't, so why did you force it upon yourself? For money? For love?
For respectability? Oh, how confusing our choices get when we are already
confused. If we could hug and forgive our past selves, imagine how good
that would feel.)

Or maybe you do remember.

Maybe it happened all of a sudden. Maybe you took the pushing, the shoving,
the piling on, the compression of you, the compression of your soul into
some box they wanted to fit you in, a box with sides and a lid and they sat
on it and they sat on you, and you wondered how long you could breathe
in that box and whether you should poke air holes, and you made excuses
for them and you remembered how they had been so nice to you in the past
and you thought, "Maybe they will stop. Maybe this is a dream. Maybe they
will just let me be again."

Until you realized they wouldn't. The pressure would always be there.
And you were not meant to exist in so small of a box, even with air holes.
continued ...

Then you knew that you could live with yourself only if you stood up and said the things you wanted to say.

The secret things.

The things that burned in your soul. The words that woke you at night and made you sweat without a barbell or a run. The feelings that, if you did not let them be heard, if you did not let the words rise to the surface of the ocean of you, you knew these words would become rocks.

Heavy rocks.

Like the rocks that lined the pockets of Virginia Woolf when she walked into that river in that heavy, heavy coat and let herself slip under the water. When she stopped holding her breath, and she let the water fill her lungs where air used to be. And her lungs could not use that water, and she sank. And she died.

That could be you. That would be you. So you dumped the rocks. You let the words out. You rose to the surface. You breathed again.

And you lived.

And that's when the old you ended. And when you were born again. But not in the way of the church or a religion. There was no white light and no priest. No baptism in a cool pool. No songs by a choir with swaying robes. You were simply and wholly born again in the way of you.

And that was enough.

Because you were born to live, not just exist.

≫

You Don't Suck As Much As You Think You Do

If you're going to get better at fitness (or anything), then you need to accept one fact: You do not suck as much as you think you do.

Most of us are far harder on ourselves than anyone else ever could be. We look at other people and compare ourselves, often to our own detriment.

But here's the thing: you're not going to last very long if you keep thinking you're the worst. There's only so long you can punch yourself in the mental face before you just say "Screw this" and walk away, off to try something else, then something else, and something else.

We do this to ourselves, though -- this "you suck" mentality. And our culture helps. Plus, there's money to be made by telling us we suck, because there's always someone to teach us how to improve. That's okay (we live in a capitalistic society), but nobody's going to regulate this talk, so you need to learn to regulate yourself.

Because people (with good intentions) will say this:
"Look at this you're bad at. And this. And this."
"Work your goats. Work your goats. Work your goats."

But it gets old, and it has a cost.

I know because I used to be this way. All my life, I was the first one in the line to punch myself in the mental face because I wasn't the best at this or that. I'd compare myself to him or her or even to some person I'd never met. My goats were many. They multiplied daily. And they ran all over my backyard, obscuring any flowers, hiding any accomplishments. CrossFit only helped me see more goats. Oh, those goats. I chased those ugly, smelly things constantly.

Then, one day, I realized I was spending all my time herding goats, and I was not enjoying the things I did like and I was good at. So I opened the gates. I let all the goats run free. And then I could see the flowers again. Life was a heck of a lot more beautiful ... and FUN.

And now? The goats hang around the outer edges of the lawn, but I don't let them eat the flowers and sometimes I just run right at them. Goats don't bother me so much anymore.

Do I still suck at some things? Yes. But I don't give a damn anymore. I work on some things to improve -- like double-unders or snatches. And some things I just let run into the woods. Handstand walking? I don't care. I don't want to do it, and my chiropractor begs me not to do it. It doesn't matter to my physical or mental well-being if I do it. I'm not a professional athlete. I'm not a local competitor. I'm just a writer who wants to stay healthy and move heavy weight, and I'm never going to walk on my hands. I'm good with that.

What I realized finally was that in beating myself up all the time about my shortcomings, I was creating a miserable life for myself. I was getting better at some tasks, but at a huge mental cost. For my objectives, it wasn't worth it.

Does this make me weak? Some people might say so. But guess what? I don't care. They don't live in my skin. I do. And I'm happy.

Not Too Much To Ask

I try to live my life so that in the imaginary movie trailer of my existence there is not one scene where I grab my hair and cry out, "My God, what have I done?"

Nor do I want that scene where the guitar strums slowly as the camera pulls back from the roadway wreckage.

And please, not one scene where my wide-eyed children shake a drunken or drug-addicted me awake in a living room or a hospital, asking in high-pitched voices, "Mom, what happened?"

No, I don't want the music montage of my life over the years to show progression only from great promise to unfulfilled promise.

I don't want to be unfulfilled at anything. I want to be full and happy, and still loony enough to laugh loud enough that I make other people laugh.

I don't need millions of dollars. I don't need 60 pairs of shoes. I don't want too much of anything except love.

I don't think it's too much to ask.

And I imagine you want the same things, when you really think about it. I imagine that we are not that different after all.

Wear Out Your Boots On The High Road

When you are angry or sad or disappointed, think before you say or post anything.

Think before you buy a ticket on the Public Hurt Train. There are many passengers there and they will welcome you, but the cost of the ticket is much higher than it initially appears.

Instead, in your darkest moments, think of how to help others, not merely yourself. Think of how you can help them, instead of them helping you. It sounds crazy, but believe me when I say that this turn can save you from many regrets.

Be grateful for the ears of others, but be cautious.

Be true to yourself, but be mindful.

Ask for help if you need it, but give help too.

The more good you put into this world, the more good that will come back to you. It's sappy but it's true. I've seen it. So have you.

Don't fight darkness with darkness unless there is absolutely no other way and you have worn out your boots on the high road. Be bleeding and broken before you fold your fingers into that fist.

Revenge is bitter, and should be the last taste you seek.

Everyday Superheroes

I can't will it out of you.

I can't pull the effort from you. I can't tug on your heart and make this beautiful accomplishment appear, like a magician popping a bouquet of flowers from my closed hand.

I wish I could. If there was a way, I'd do the work of 10 women just to give nine people a break for a little while. I was born with extra energy; I should get to share it like that.

But I can't. You have to bring it.

You have to conjure the fire and the drive, you have to build the passion, you have to fan your own flame from a few sparks. You might think you can't. You're tired, you have a lot of responsibilities; life (and everyone you know) needs so much from you.

But, oh, you have wells within you that you have not even begun to tap. Depth and darkness that carry so much power and energy that whole cities could be lit from your current, if we all lived in some superhero land.

But we're not superheroes, and the women of wonder live in our hearts. But maybe that's enough. Maybe you and I and these words and these barbells are the start of something kind of fabulous. Maybe. There's only one way to know for sure. Try. And, then, if it works, if your life is better because you started moving your body and lifting your life, tell the others. Tell them all. Don't leave anybody behind.

»

Beyond Broken

We are all broken. Show me someone who says they are perfectly unharmed and I'm looking at a liar, or someone trying desperately to put up a brave front.

None of us get through life in an inviolate state. There is no one left unscathed; only those who have managed to bounce back quicker or higher.

Yet we find our sanctuaries. Places that help us to heal, to put ourselves back together, to make us stronger, to grow the scars over the wounds. For some of us, that place is the gym. For some of us, solace is found in a workout.

As odd as it seems, we heal somehow through this fire. Like a heat that cauterizes the wound, the new pain takes the old pain away.

We go deeper into the darkness in order to escape and free ourselves.

We go through in order to get through, to emerge on the other side into the light, to fall in triumph and exhaustion and some kind of gratitude that such light even exists.

We don't want to escape for just right now, we want to go beyond and leave the pain, make it a memory, abandon it like a sandbag after the run, a barbell after the workout, an empty water bottle.

We used that pain, and now we can walk away from it.

continued ...

It makes no sense to the others, the people outside our circle, who don't understand. If you've anesthetized yourself to life, it's hard to understand what the raw edges feel like, the grittiness, the harsh reality.

It's hard to understand that the tight cornering and jarring ride of the sports car is somehow preferable to the cushioned, soft travel of the sedan.

It's hard to understand that you can feel discomfort without being consumed by it, and that it somehow helps you to find your way.

But we know. And, hopefully, we're moving beyond broken with every workout and every day.

Your Genius

We're taught that some people are special, and that some people aren't.
We're taught that some folks are geniuses, and that most of us are not.
What a bunch of hooey. It's not as simple as that.

Yes, some people have physical attributes or mental acuity that the rest
of us do not. Certainly. I will never dunk a basketball and you may never
invent a new language.

That doesn't mean we're not special. That doesn't mean we're not gifted.
That doesn't mean anyone is better than us.

Don't believe the hype.

The genius does not reside in anyone else more than it resides in you.
Because genius doesn't have to be a certain mass of neurons or the ability
to score high on an IQ test. Genius originally meant "a person's natural
ability" -- only in the last few centuries did we change the definition to
indicate exceptional ability.

Hence, maybe your genius is what you are here to do, to make, to create,
to live. Some people never figure this out. It's not an easy task. Sometimes,
it takes a lifetime. I do not exaggerate when I say that it's taken me almost
fifty years and I'm not certain I know what I'm doing. I believe Vincent
Van Gogh died not knowing he had it right.

There is no guarantee, no great reveal, no obvious sign when you hit upon the right answer for you. No button lights up, no music starts, no clouds part. No angels sing.

After much pain, there is simply less pain. And, if you are extremely lucky, more love.

But this is how you know that you are where you should be, that you are doing what you should do, that you have stumbled upon that which must be part of your life. This is how you know you have found your own genius.

I urge you to clear the distractions from your eyes and your soul, to immerse yourself in the truth that doesn't falter, to learn to listen for the notes that are always in tune. They are deep in your being and they scare you. I know. I get that. But they are the music you must bring forth if you would truly live, truly breathe, truly be.

Your genius awaits you. You are special. But it is up to you to figure out exactly how.

This Cloud Will Not Last Forever

You can't rely on happiness or positive thinking.

Happiness isn't a truck that makes regular deliveries. Sometimes it skips whole neighborhoods, or doesn't show up for a year, making people think it will never come again. And maybe it won't. But it's better to keep your front door open or an ear tilted for the sound, just because you never really know, you know?

Still, relying on happiness is a fool's game.

So too is relying on sadness, although you will always win that game. Sadness is the constant of the world.

Better to greet both happiness and sadness when they come.
(Your greeting will not affect their arrival or their departure.)

They will each sit for a while. And they will leave then they are ready.

You know this, but it helps to be reminded.

The cloud is not permanent. But neither is the sunshine. Once you can see the comfort in both of them, you will cease to worry about the weather.

The Way Out Of The Woods

Most people do not intend to hurt us. I truly believe that most people are like you and me -- working hard to do the right thing but screwing up here and messing up there. None of us is perfect, or even close to a shadow of perfect. We are all so human. Flawed, wonderful, beautiful humans.

Remember this when you find yourself in a cloud of pain: try to keep your bearings amidst the confusion. Assigning blame or divining malice will help no one here. Blame is the most temporary of balms. It feels good for a moment, and then its healing power is over and it sits like a gooey mess on the wound, doing nothing but obscuring the skin and delaying the process by which you will heal.

But what do you do? What path do you take to get out of that cloud of pain? To find your way again? To get back on the path that felt like it was going somewhere exotic, before you took a sudden turn and found yourself in the brambles, scratched and bleeding and crying?

You do what they told you to do as a child. Stand still and wait for someone to arrive. Stop crying, assess your surroundings, keep warm ... and wait. This is not a rescue you need, but simply human contact. Someone to orient you, to offer a hand and say, "Hey, I'm here. You're going to be okay." That might be all you need to keep going. A helper. Someone to pick you up off your keister, brush the dirt from your face, and say, "It's going to be all right."

continued ...

We all need that, whether we want to admit it or not. For all our love of independence, for all our glorification of the great American "go it alone" myth, in our most scared, sacred, real, basic selves we need connection. Human connection.

Someone once said, "Our greatest need, after food and shelter, is for stories." And what are stories? Human connection. A reminder that we are not alone, that we are never really alone, no matter how alone we feel.

When you feel scared and lost, remember this: we all are. And most of us are ready and willing (and happy) to lend a hand, pull you off your keister, and wipe the dirt from your face so that you can keep going. If I do it for you, you'll do it for the next person, and we'll all find our way out of the woods some day.

What The Barbell Took

It started as a way to calm the angry voice inside.

The part in your head that was furious because life wasn't perfect and did not seem like it ever would be. That's how you met the barbell. You had to get the angry voice out. You tried other stuff -- running, cycling, maybe even beer -- but the voice always came back. So you started in on the barbell, and then something happened.

When nothing else seemed to work right, the barbell felt right. You could swear, stomp, smash, and get all sorts of ugly but the barbell just took it. Took all of it. All your abuse, your hatred, your ugliness -- took it all and never talked back. Never made you feel small. Never told you to smile and play nice. It was okay to be angry with the barbell, even preferred sometimes.

The barbell made you feel big, no matter how short or tiny or less than powerful you felt. Once that barbell was in your callused hands with some bumpers on the ends, you were ten feet tall and had an ass that could squat the world. The barbell, used well, gave you power. And you liked it.

Then, somewhere in your braying about your lifts and your experience that you just couldn't shut up about, the angry voice stopped. Vanished into the muggy night. Left. Beat it out of town. And the cool quiet that was left? Stunning in its peace.

You still pulled up the voice sometimes, conjured the edge, the grit, the bite when you needed to make things happen, but your anger was a pale comparison to what it was before. A faded glory. A bon homage to the fury of youth.

The barbell took that angry voice and gave you a new one. And everyone wondered why you sounded so happy.

Except those who had met the barbell too.

Approval Is Overrated

Don't wait for approval.

So many people make this mistake in life: they hesitate to act bold and beautiful because they're just not sure. They're waiting for someone to tell them "Yes!" or "Do it" or "That's it, Sweetie!"

Well, forget that. Sweetie's all grown up and she's got a barbell in her hands. She knows what she needs to do. She just needs to flipping do it.

Stop waiting for permission to live your life, or do what you really want to do. You get one go-round. One. You can be brave and risk your heart and breath and love a million times a day ... or you can play it safe and make sure that you're doing the right thing before you do it.

You can hesitate and come in second, or fifth, or fifteenth, or fiftieth. Or, worse, never even start -- because you weren't quite sure it was the right thing to do.

Yes, you might get hurt. Yes, you might screw up. Who cares? Only you and your big ego. So get over yourself and lay your heart on the line every day. Be brave. Be big. And, whenever you can, be kind. It's far more important than any of us ever realize.

Don't wait for approval. Go out and be exactly who you want to be.

The Point Of Diminishing Returns

We all reach this point at some moment in our lives, in our work or our routine or our relationship, even if we don't want to admit it. (And we usually don't want to admit it.) The point where the pain is more than the pleasure, much more.

What started out as fun is now barely enjoyable. A few moments of joy here and there, interrupted (no, dominated) by long stretches of something more than unpleasantness. Something closer to what feels like penance for some unnamed sin, a purgatory more than an actual agony.

Agony would be easier to turn a cold shoulder to, easier to walk away from. You would want to leave agony.

No, this funk is more like a low-grade fever, a persistent ache, a dull pain that never quite doubles you ever but doesn't go away either.

This is the point of diminishing returns, and you have two choices here. Find a way to improve, or find a way out.

continued ...

Ignore and endure is not a sound option. You can choose it (many people do), but popularity is not justification. Yes, some parts of life are grin and bear it, things to be survived, but if your entire life feels like survival, something is wrong. I suggest you find the parts that don't fit well, and then figure out a plan.

Because life should not be seen as something you endure. Life is not called Endurance. Nay, life is meant to be *lived*.

And to do that you need passion and joy.

Diminishing returns is not a good plan for your finances or your life. Diminishing returns leave you feeling diminished. So find a better place to invest, whether that means in another or in yourself. But do something. Waiting it out is simply giving away your one and only life.

Untapped Oceans

People talk about potential, but no one knows your potential.
You barely know it yourself.

But you do know your imagined limits, your perceived weaknesses,
and all the horrid little words you tell yourself in the smallest moments.
They're not true, but they feel true and so you speak them in your mind.

What if you stopped saying bullshit to yourself? What could you accomplish?

Perhaps this thought frightens you. Perhaps your potential scares you.
I know my potential scares me. The thought of that which I could be
capable of is a frightening prospect. Maybe you are the same.

Take a moment, and really think about yourself and your dreams. What if
you spoke those dreams out loud? What if you tried and failed? Would you
live? Would you still breathe? Would you still walk this earth? And if so,
then what exactly are you waiting for?

Stop stopping yourself.
Stop limiting yourself.
Stop fortifying your imaginary walls.

L.D.

Break through your own bullshit. If you don't, you will never be free. Is that acceptable to you? Is it okay to live half your life? Is it okay to die with your dreams unspoken? I'm guessing that's probably not what you want.

Remember: failing is okay. Not reaching all of your goals? You'll live with that. We all live with that, every single one of us.

But to not try? To stop short because you got scared? That memory will haunt you until your last breath escapes your lungs.

So, get out there and blow past your own boundaries.

There are oceans in me, untapped.
Rivers of strength I have yet to ride down.
Caverns of persistence that I have yet to explore.
And there is love in me that knows no bounds.

Get Out Of Your Own Way

If you offer truth, and in return are offered lies, walk away. There are better places for you to be.

I don't say this to sadden you, but to offer a view of your heart, of your mind, of you that maybe you have forgotten.

You are not a discount item. You are not a damaged good. You don't have to take what anyone gives you.

No, thank you. Not now. Not this time. All of these statements are acceptable answers. Say them and press onward.

Because if you cannot trust another person to be truthful, why are you talking to them? Are you willing to become untruthful? Are you willing to lose your self-respect?

If you are willing to sacrifice your integrity, do these things. I will be sad if you do, but that is not your concern. You must live your life and you must live it your way, not my way or the way of anyone else. For me to suggest what you should do is as preposterous as for you to suggest my path. Yet, we still do this, because we are human and we are compelled to share our experiences. Maybe, in these experiences, there is knowledge for others to gain. I do not know this for sure, but I hope this for certain.

continued ...

Convince yourself that the end justifies the means, if that is the path you must choose. Sleep with that under your pillow.

Or, even better, quiet the noisy distractions of this world and listen to your inner self, the voice that speaks so softly you do not always hear it. You know the answer before you ask yourself the question. Listen, and then get out of your own way.

If you offer truth, and in return are offered lies, walk away. There are better places for you to be.

How To Survive Almost Anything

1. Swallow your pride and ask for help.

2. Learn to accept the help you asked for.

3. Do not become addicted to help. Regain your strength and independence.

4. Laugh. Even in the face of the worst thing ever, manage a chuckle somewhere. It is the only way to know for sure that your spirit still can rise. You'll be surprised at how good it will feel.

5. Lift. You probably thought I would put "love" here, right? But you already love, I know that. You know that. Your survival is so inherently built on your capacity to love that telling you to love would be akin to saying you need to breathe air.

No, you need to be reminded to lift. Why? Because in our heaviest times, we need to be reminded in a very physical way that there is weight on us. We live with mental weight that we can only see with our minds. Put that weight in a physical form in front of us, however, and force us to lift it. Now we know that weight can be put on and taken off -- just like those bumpers on the barbell. And it is up to us to figure out how to take that mental weight off ourselves. Sometimes, we need the help of professionals, like a coach. Sometimes we need the help of a friend to make our task easier. And sometimes we need no one but us. One pair of hands and one mind. We can go on.

L.D.

Creating Problems That Don't Exist

Here's one of the simplest pieces of advice I can give anyone, including myself: Don't create problems that don't exist.

You probably have enough situations that need to be dealt with. You don't need new problems. Yet you see one here and there and over there.

Or maybe you don't.

Maybe your ego sees those problems. Maybe your brain just made up that situation. Maybe you're the only one seeing shadows in a gorgeous field of sunshine.

I always liked this statement: "Do not ascribe to malice that which can be explained by stupidity." Or as my mother would say, "She just doesn't have a lot upstairs. Bless her." (My mother is far kinder than I am.)

But the point here is that unless you're an attorney looking for malice, why assume it?

We assume malice because it makes us feel smart. Detecting malice and motive makes us amateur detectives, and stringing together clues makes us perceptive. Pointing out flaws or faults or errors is its own form of ego massage. "We see the problem! Listen to us!" We feel like we have solved a puzzle, except sometimes there was no puzzle to solve. We invented an answer to a question that hadn't been asked.

People often assume the person arguing hardest, or speaking the fastest, or using the most multi-syllabic words is the smartest. Often, this theory is wrong. The smartest person may have assessed and walked away. They had more important things to do. They saw the fallacy of the argument. They recognized the time suck that should be avoided like the quicksand it is. They kept walking.

Fools create problems that do not exist. Fools fight wars that no one else started. Fools busy themselves with the foolish.

Look and see what is there. Do not try so hard to see what is not. Deal with problems that exist, but avoid creating problems that do not exist.

You Can't Overachieve

There are many stupid words in our lexicon, but let's talk about this one:
Overachiever.

Overachiever: someone who achieves too much, or achieves more than
they were expected to. How stupid is that? Like you're only supposed to
achieve so much, and then you've gone too far? Like someone else gets to
determine what you should achieve?

Who came up with that word? And why do we insist on using it?

I never even knew that word existed until I was in my 20's. We just achieved
in my family, as much as we could as often as we could. Achievement was
the result of hard work. We were good with that. Go hard and get results.
What part of that formula needs changing? No part. Zero. Nada. Zilch.
And guess what? There's no limit on achieving. No quota, no tariff, no mark
you cannot go above.

You can achieve as much as you want.

Holy hell. What a concept, right?

continued ...

Except there are these fools who make up words like "overachiever" so
that you are supposed to feel bad if you achieve "too" much. It's supposedly
not cool. Well, forget cool then! I'm going to do what I want to do.
And you get to do the same. You want to achieve, I'm good with that.
You don't want to achieve anything? Well, I'm good with that too … as long
as you don't affect me or what I'm doing. Like Chrissie Hynde of the
Pretenders sang: "I got a smile for everyone I meet. As long as you don't
try dragging my bay, or dropping the bomb on my street." (I don't have a bay
-- you may not either -- but I think we can safely assume we're taking
a ride in Metaphor Land on this one. We understand what she's saying.)

Anyhow, my point is this: Go do your thing, and stop listening to morons.
There is no such thing as overachieving. There is only the reality of kicking
ass and making awesome happen. Let the bystanders figure it out and put
names on everything. Hard workers are too busy achieving.

Everything Changes But The Truth

I once had a job. Other people called it a dream job -- maybe I thought of it
that way too, at times. It used my skills, paid well, allowed me to travel
the world, and gave me a modicum of internet fame. Wonderful people
wanted to befriend me, and I loved the community that came with that job.

It also affected several relationships, moved me away from my mom, and
sometimes allowed me the freedom to indulge the pompous ass who lives
under my skin no matter how hard I try to get rid of her. All of this is true,
and none of it is easy to admit.

I don't have that job anymore.

One day, I walked into work and they handed me some paperwork and
told me to gather my things. I was no longer needed by them.

I filled a box and went home to my family.

Life went on. The wind kept blowing. The ocean never missed a wave.
No walruses beached themselves. People still ordered overpriced coffee
with too much steamed milk and then sat down at wooden tables and
stared at metal and plastic devices instead of the human flesh and blood
in front of them.

The things we experience in our lives are both the most important, amazing, pertinent things in the history of the universe and absolutely nothing at the same exact time. If we breathe, we survive. If our lungs fill with air, we go on. The heart is a strong muscle.

Fill your cup. Drink it down. Get another.

The wind keeps blowing.

And some where, in some gym, some one picks up a barbell.

Worth

People speak of worth like they know what worth is.

"He's worth $350 million." "She's worth $1.2 billion."
You have told me nothing except what a bank would value.

I am not a bank. Neither are you. Thank goodness.

Worth in dollars is a standard measuring unit that puts a value on what
is seen, on what can be measured.

Who wants that?
Some people. Business people. And shallow people.

Still, I know I cannot eat air or good intentions or books.
You know that too.

And yet I find more measure of a woman (or man) in what she will do
and won't do, in where she draws the line, in when she raises her voice,
in when she drops her hand. Worth. Value. Ability. Merit. So many words
to measure that which perhaps cannot be measured.

So, don't stress. Just work. Try to help others rise along with yourself.

You'll be amazed at how your worth will increase in both what can and
cannot be measured.

The World Is Brutal And You Must Be Brave

The world is brutal, and you must be brave.

I wish I could tell you otherwise. I wish I could fill your days with new barbells and love and inspiring personal records. I wish I could tell you that the path to success is shiny and bright, and sunshine will come out of your sweet patootie.

But that's not going to happen. And you should probably stop listening to the people who feed you this bullshit. The world is a much darker place. There are no unicorns, only horses with points glued to their noses. The world can be a cold and vicious place, seemingly devoid of real meaning. You can lose yourself in the world, searching again and again for soul.

But don't.

There is soul and you know how to look for it. You must look for it. You must find it. Just because the world is brutal doesn't mean that you get to hide yourself off from it and live the life of the complainer, the person who never gets a break, the whiner with the perpetually doomed viewpoint, certain that life's sucker-punch is always headed for them. Don't search for pity. Don't settle for consolation. Fight for victory.

Salvation sits right at your feet.

continued ...

It's just a stupid barbell, but it's one kick-ass weapon against the darkness. Against the brutality of the world. Against the brutality of your own thoughts. Pick it up and the world gets better, at least in your own mind.

And that's where everything starts, doesn't it? Change is born of one person, one mind, one action. Somebody who says "Yeah, this sucks but I'm not going down. I am so much stronger than you know!"

The world is brutal and you must be brave.

But you have a barbell. You can do something. And then another thing. And another. You change. Things change. We change. Get on it.

Joy Is Contagious

Your ability to be happy for the success of others is more important than you know.

This thought is not new, but it merits almost daily iteration: Your joy for the joy of others is essential to your own joy. Understand that. Breathe it in.

Think about it this way: Joy does not stand independently. It is not something aloof and unrelated. Joy does not sit in its own chair in the coffee shop, hesitant to talk to anybody. Joy isn't buried in their phone screen.

Joy is contagious. Joy is infectious. Most of the time, you can't help catching it. Joy pulls up a chair. Joy talks too loud and hugs too long and too much. Joy spreads, if you let it.

So let it.

Joy will jump from one person to another, but it can't pass itself. Joy needs a carrier.

Joy needs you.

L.D.

But we so often get confused by the nature of joy. We think joy is the sexy gal we have to seduce by playing cool, by watching out of the corner of our eye, by posing across the room.

Not exactly.

Joy wants you to be joyful. Joy needs expression to spread. Joy is waiting to go to the prom with the person brave enough to ask her. But joy needs you to ask. Joy needs you to get out of your chair, get off your phone, and come alive.

So do that. Spread joy. Your own fortune will change.

What If You Had Guts Like That?

Three weeks before I was laid off, I bought a new car. The license plate frame from the dealer read "Be Happy." It might as well have said, "Hold on! The ride is going to get really bumpy but you'll survive!"

None of us are guaranteed anything in this life, and maybe that's why we struggle to find security. This job, that house, this partner. "If something happens, I'll be okay." We hedge our bets, we worry, we settle. That's kind of sad, isn't it?

Yet we all do it to some extent. Our fear of the unknown sometimes propels us to settle for some crappy knowns. Like that old saying: "Better the devil you know than the devil you don't." But what if you didn't believe that?

What if you decided to take what was unseen, or you chose the deal behind the curtain? What if you had guts like that? What if the devil you don't know is a hell of lot better than the devil you do? And what if he's not a devil at all?

People say, "Perception is reality." I say "Perception is reality for idiots." What we perceive isn't always what is. Magicians aren't the only ones practicing sleight of hand.

Look for yourself. Decide for yourself. And, sometimes, take the bird that's not in your hand. Run after the ones in the bush. Maybe you'll only make noise and scare the birds away, but oh they'll look so beautiful as they soar against the azure sky.

L.D.

It's A Great Life If You Don't Weaken

When I was a kid, often my mother would say, "It's a great life if you don't weaken." Back then, I never really understood what she meant. I was young, and life looked pretty damn awesome. But as I aged, I understood her words more and more with each passing year.

We all start out strong. Almost every one of us came into this world with a loud cry announcing: "I am here and I want attention!"

Sometimes we got that attention, and sometimes we didn't. Such is life. And so life seeds the crop of broken hearts that we try to fill with bourbon or running or barbells or any of the pursuits we adopt to fill all those hours when human connection is not available or not enough. We call these things hobbies or convince ourselves that they are important to our well-being of body or mind or spirit, but like almost everything we adopt in this life, they are also a way to fill what can never be filled: Something inside us that needs another soul to say, "I see you. And I understand." If only things could do this for us, but they cannot, and so we need other humans.

continued ...

The trouble with this world is this world. That fact alone is both depressing and uplifting.

We hold our salvation, but we so often do not understand it. Yet we need to understand human connection and grasp it like it is the last piece of driftwood in a rapidly moving stream. Connection is your chance at survival. Grab that human connection and keep your chin above the surface of the aggressive water so long as you have the strength. Keep bobbing up. Ride the current. Get a breath here and there. It sounds hard -- it is hard -- but all we really have is this moment, each other, and love.

This world beats us down, even the strongest of us, and we get weary. But here's the thing: it happens to all of us. We all feel that way. We just don't like to admit it. We hate to admit need. We hate to appear needy.

But imagine how life could be if you just said this: "I need your help."

And imagine how life could be if your reply to someone else was simply this: "I'd be happy to help."

Another piece of wood pops up in the stream. Grab it.

It's a great life if you don't weaken.

STRONG STARTS IN THE MIND

22428970R00080

Made in the USA
Middletown, DE
30 July 2015